JAMES HERRIOT'S

Treasury of Inspirational Stories for Children

Warm and Joyful Tales
by the Author of *All Creatures Great and Small*

Illustrations by Ruth Brown
and Peter Barrett

ST. MARTIN'S GRIFFIN ⚜ NEW YORK

JAMES HERRIOT'S TREASURY OF INSPIRATIONAL STORIES FOR CHILDREN

Moses the Kitten: © 1974, 1984 The James Herriot Partnership
Illustrations © 1984 Peter Barrett
Only One Woof: © 1974, 1985 The James Herriot Partnership
Illustrations © 1985 Peter Barrett
The Christmas Day Kitten: © 1976, 1986 The James Herriot Partnership
Illustrations © 1986 Ruth Brown
Bonny's Big Day: © 1972, 1987 The James Herriot Partnership
Illustrations © 1988 Ruth Brown
Blossom Comes Home: © 1972, 1988 The James Herriot Partnership
Illustrations © 1988 Ruth Brown
The Market Square Dog: © 1989 The James Herriot Partnership
Illustrations © 1988 Ruth Brown
Oscar, Cat-About-Town: © 1977, 1990 The James Herriot Partnership
Illustrations © 1990 Ruth Brown
Smudge, the Little Lost Lamb: © 1991 The James Herriot Partnership
Illustrations © 1991 Ruth Brown

www.stmartins.com

Library of Congress Cataloging-in-Publication Data

Herriot, James.
   James Herriot's treasury of inspirational stories for children/ James Herriot.
      p. cm.
   Summary: A collection of the author's stories for children, including "Moses the Kitten," "The Market Square Dog," and "Smudge, the Little Lost Lamb."
   ISBN 0-312-34972-6
   EAN 978-0-312-34972-1
   1. Pets—England—Yorkshire—Biography—Juvenile literature. 2. Domestic animals—England—Yorkshire—Biography—Juvenile literature. 3. Farm life—England—Yorkshire—Juvenile literature. [1. Animals. 2. Farm life.] I. Title. II. Title: Treasury of inspirational stories for children.

SF416.2.H45 1992
636—dc20

92-24036
CIP
AC

Originally published under the title *James Herriot's Treasury for Children*

First St. Martin's Griffin Edition: October 2005

10 9 8 7 6 5 4 3 2 1

CONTENTS

Moses the Kitten

Illustrated by Peter Barrett

There have been times in the winter when I
have regretted being a vet and this looked like
one of them.

I had driven about ten miles from home, thinking
all the time that the Dales always looked their
coldest, not when they were covered with snow,
but as now, when the first sprinkling streaked the bare
flanks of the fells in bars of black and white like the
ribs of a crouching beast. And now in front of me
was a farm gate rattling on its hinges as the wind
shook it.

The car, heaterless and draughty as it was, seemed like a haven in an uncharitable world and I gripped the wheel tightly with my woollen-gloved hands for a few moments before opening the door. The wind almost tore the handle from my fingers as I got out but I managed to crash the door shut before stumbling over the frozen mud to the gate. Muffled as I was in heavy coat and scarf pulled up to my ears I could feel the icy gusts biting at my face, whipping up my nose and hammering painfully into the air spaces in my head.

I had driven through and, streaming-eyed, was about to get back into the car when I noticed something unusual. There was a frozen pond just off the path and among the rime-covered rushes which fringed the dead opacity of the surface a small object stood out, shiny black.

I went over and looked closer. It was a tiny kitten, probably about six weeks old, huddled and immobile, eyes tightly closed. Bending down, I poked gently at the furry body. It must be dead; a morsel like this couldn't possibly survive in such cold
. . . but no,
there was a spark of life because the mouth opened soundlessly for a second then closed.

Quickly I lifted the little creature and tucked it inside my coat. As I drove into the farmyard I called to the farmer who was carrying two buckets out of the calf house. ''I've got one of your kittens here, Mr Butler. It must have strayed outside.''

Mr Butler put down his buckets and looked blank. *''Kitten?* We haven't got no kittens at present.''

I showed him my find and he looked more puzzled.

''Well that's a rum 'un, there's no black cats on this spot. We've all sorts o' colours but no black 'uns.''

''Well he must have come from somewhere else,'' I said. ''Though I can't imagine anything so small travelling very far. It's rather mysterious.''

I held the kitten out and he engulfed it with his big, work-roughened hand.
"Poor little beggar, he's only just alive.
I'll take him into t'house and see if the missus can do owt for him."

In the farm kitchen Mrs Butler was all concern. "Oh what a shame!" She smoothed back the bedraggled hair with one finger. "And it's got such a pretty face." She looked up at me. "What is it, anyway, a him or a her?"

I took a quick look behind the hind legs. "It's a Tom."

"Right," she said. "I'll get some warm milk into him but first of all we'll give him the old cure."

She went over to the fireside oven on the big black kitchen range, opened the door and popped him inside.

I smiled. It was the classical procedure when new-born lambs were found suffering from cold and exposure; into the oven they went and the results were often dramatic. Mrs Butler left the door partly open and I could just see the little black figure inside; he didn't seem to care much what was happening to him.

The next hour I spent in the byre wrestling with the hind feet of a cow. The cleats were overgrown and grossly misshapen and upturned, causing the animal to hobble along on her heels. My job was to pare and hack away the excess horn and my long held opinion that the hind feet of a cow were never meant to be handled by man was thoroughly confirmed. We had a rope round the hock and the leg pulled up over a beam in the roof but the leg still pistoned back and forth while I hung on till my teeth rattled. By the time I had finished the sweat was running into my eyes and I had quite forgotten the cold day outside.

Still, I thought, as I eased the kinks from my spine
when I had finished, there were compensations.
There was a satisfaction in the sight of the cow
standing comfortably on two almost normal
looking feet.

"Well that's summat like," Mr Butler grunted.
"Come in the house and wash your hands."

In the kitchen as I bent over the brown earthenware sink I kept glancing across at the oven.

Mrs Butler laughed. "Oh he's still with us. Come and have a look."

It was difficult to see the kitten in the dark interior but when I spotted him I put out my hand and touched him and he turned his head towards me.

"He's coming round," I said. "That hour in there has worked wonders."

"Doesn't often fail." The farmer's wife lifted him out. "I think he's a little tough 'un." She began to spoon warm milk into the tiny mouth.

"I reckon we'll have him lappin' in a day or two."

"You're going to keep him, then?"

"Too true we are. I'm going to call him Moses."

"*Moses?*"

"Aye, you found him among the rushes, didn't you?"

I laughed. "That's right. It's a good name."

I was on the Butler farm about a fortnight later and I kept looking around for Moses. Farmers rarely have their cats indoors and I thought that if the black kitten had survived he would have joined the feline colony around the buildings.

Farm cats have a pretty good time. They may not be petted or cosseted but it has always seemed to me that they lead a free, natural life. They are expected to catch mice but if they are not so inclined there is abundant food at hand; bowls of milk here and there and the dogs' dishes to be raided if anything interesting is left over.

I had seen plenty of cats around today,
some flitting nervously away, others friendly
and purring. There was a tabby loping gracefully
across the cobbles and a big tortoise-shell was curled
on a bed of straw at the warm
end of the byre; cats are
connoisseurs of
comfort.

When Mr Butler went to fetch some hot water I had a quick look in the bullock house and a white Tom regarded me placidly from between the bars of a hay rack where he had been taking a siesta. But there was no sign of Moses.

I finished drying my arms and was about to make a casual reference to the kitten when Mr Butler handed me my jacket.

"Come round here with me if you've got a minute," he said.

"I've got summat to show you."

I followed him through the door at the end and across a passage into the long, low-roofed piggery. He stopped at a pen about half way down and pointed inside.

"Look 'ere," he said.

I leaned over the wall and my face must have shown my astonishment because the farmer burst into a shout of laughter.

"That's summat new for you, isn't it?"

I stared unbelievingly down at a large sow stretched comfortably on her side, suckling a litter of about twelve piglets and right in the middle of the long pink row, furry black and incongruous, was *Moses*. He had a teat in his mouth and was absorbing his nourishment with the same rapt enjoyment as his smooth-skinned fellows on either side.

''What the devil . . .?'' I gasped.

Mr Butler was still laughing. ''I thought you'd never have seen anything like that before, I never have, any road.''

''But how did it happen?'' I still couldn't drag my eyes away.

''It was the Missus's idea,'' he replied. ''When she'd got the little youth lappin' milk she took him out to find a right warm spot for him in the buildings. She settled on this pen because the sow, Bertha, had just had a litter and I had a heater in and it was grand and cosy.''

I nodded. ''Sounds just right.''

Well she put Moses and a bowl of milk in here,'' the farmer went on, ''but the little feller didn't stay by the heater very long — next time I looked in he was round at t'milk bar.''

I shrugged my shoulders. ''They say you see something new every day at this game, but this is something I've never even heard of. Anyway, he looks well on it — does he actually live on the sow's milk or does he still drink from his bowl?''

''A bit of both, I reckon. It's hard to say.''

Anyway, whatever mixture Moses was getting he grew rapidly into a sleek, handsome animal with an unusually high gloss to his coat which may or may not have been due to the porcine element of his diet.

I never went to the Butlers' without having a look in the pig pen. Bertha, his foster mother, seemed to find nothing unusual in this hairy intruder and pushed him around casually with pleased grunts just as she did with the rest of her brood.

Moses for his part appeared to find the society of the pigs very congenial. When the piglets curled up together and settled down for a sleep Moses would be somewhere in the heap and when his young colleagues were weaned at eight weeks he showed his attachment to Bertha by spending most of his time with her.

And it stayed that way over the years. Often he would be right inside the pen, rubbing himself happily along the comforting bulk of the sow, but I remember him best in his favourite place; crouching on the wall looking down perhaps meditatively on what had been his first warm home.

Only One Woof

Illustrated by Peter Barrett

One nice thing about being a country vet is that there are so many interesting things to see when I visit the farms.

One sunny spring day, I visited Mr Wilkin's farm and I laughed as I watched the two sheepdog puppies playing together in the farmyard.

"Those two really love each other, don't they?"
I said.

Mr Wilkin nodded. "Aye, they are great friends.
They are never apart."

Mr Wilkin was a busy man, with many cows, pigs and sheep to look after, but he still had time for his favourite hobby – breeding and training sheepdogs. For many years, he had won silver cups all over the country. From the latest litter, he had picked the two best pups, Gyp and Sweep, and he was going to train them to run in the sheepdog trials.

The two little animals were rolling about in a happy wrestling match, growling and panting, chewing gently at each other's legs. Then suddenly they stopped playing as something else caught their attention.

"Look at that!" I cried in amazement. "They're behaving like grown-up dogs."

The pups were beginning to round up a group of tiny ducklings – much to the annoyance of the mother duck. With noses outstretched and stomachs nearly flat on the cobbles of the farmyard, they crept up on the ducklings.

"Yes," the farmer replied. "They are only twelve weeks old but their mother and father, their grandmothers and grandfathers, and away back as long as I can remember, were all sheepdogs. So these little things were born wanting to round up chickens, ducks, lambs – anything they see."

The two doggy friends were different in appearance. Sweep was black and white while Gyp was black, white and brown. But the thing you noticed most was that one of Gyp's ears stuck up while the other ear lay flat against his head. This gave him a funny, lop-sided look. In fact, he looked a bit of a clown, but he was a friendly, tail-wagging clown.

"There's one odd thing about Gyp," Mr Wilkin said. "He's never barked at all."

I looked at him in surprise. "You mean never ever?"

"That's right, not a single bark. The other dogs make a noise when strangers come to the farm, but I've never heard Gyp make a sound since he was born."

I shook my head. "How very strange. I've never heard of such a thing."

I got into my car and, as I drove away, I noticed that while Sweep and two other farm dogs barked their farewells loudly, Gyp merely wagged his tail and looked at me in a friendly manner, his pink tongue lolling out of his open mouth. A silent dog.

Some months later, just before Christmas, George Crossley, one of Mr Wilkin's oldest friends, and a very keen sheepdog trainer, came to ask if he could buy a dog as his own old dog had died. Mr Wilkin sold Sweep to him. I was a bit surprised about this because I knew that Sweep was further forward in his training than Gyp and looked like turning into a real champion. But it was Gyp he kept – perhaps it was because he just liked him. He was a funny dog with that lop-sided charm that was difficult to resist.

Gyp must have been sad to lose his brother and best friend and there was no doubt that he missed him, but there were other dogs on the farm and even if they didn't make up for Sweep, he was never really lonely. Although Gyp grew up big and strong, he wasn't quite clever enough to compete in the trials. So he just helped Mr Wilkin by herding the sheep and cattle on the farm. He was very happy to be out with his master all day, but perhaps he wondered where his doggy friend had gone.

It wasn't until the following June that I next visited the farm to see a sick cow and I saw Gyp – now fully grown – rocking along on a haycart.

I spotted him again at harvest-time, chasing rats among the stooks. He was always glad to see me, full of fun, bright-eyed and affectionate. But soundless.

There was a very long spell when none of Mr Wilkin's animals needed my help, and I did not see him or Gyp until I met them both at a sheepdog trial the following summer.

The huge field where the trial was being held was on the river's edge and the sunshine glinted on the water. The cars were drawn up along the side of the field, and groups of men, mainly competitors, stood around chatting as they watched the dogs working with the sheep. They were dressed in all sorts of clothing: cloth caps, trilbies, deer-stalkers or sometimes no hat at all; tweed jackets, best suits, open-necked shirts, fancy ties – and sometimes neither collar nor tie. Nearly all of them leaned on long crooks with the handles carved from rams' horns.

Their dogs, waiting their turn, were tied to the
fence and it was wonderful to see the long row of
waving tails and friendly expressions. Few of the dogs
knew each other but there was not a single growl,
never mind a fight.

I went over to Mr Wilkin who was leaning against his car which was parked within sight of the final pen. Gyp was tied to the bumper and was watching with interest as each dog took its turn. Mrs Wilkin was sitting on a camp stool by his side.

"Are you running a dog today, Mr Wilkin?" I asked.

"No, not this time. I've just come to watch," he replied.

I had been there for about ten minutes when suddenly the farmer lifted a pointing finger. "Look who's there!"

George Crossley with Sweep were making their way to the starting post. Gyp suddenly stiffened and sat up very straight, one ear cocked, the other flat, making him look more lop-sided than ever.

It was over a year since he had seen his brother and it seemed unlikely, I thought, that he would remember him. But he was obviously *very* interested and, as the judge waved his white handkerchief to begin the trial and the three sheep were released from the far corner of the field, Gyp rose slowly to his feet.

A gesture from Mr Crossley sent Sweep racing round the edge of the field in a wide, joyous gallop, and as he neared the sheep a whistle from Mr Crossley made him drop onto his stomach. From then on, it was easy to see that Sweep was going to be a champion as he darted and crouched at his master's commands. Short whistles, long whistles; Sweep understood them all.

No other dog all day had brought his sheep
through the three pairs of gates as easily as
Sweep did now and as he neared the final pen, it was
obvious he was going to win unless the sheep
scattered at the last moment.

George Crossley opened the gate wide and held out his crook. I could hardly hear his commands to Sweep, but his quiet words brought the dog wriggling inch by inch over the grass towards the sheep. Were they going to go bounding away and spoil everything? I held my breath. But no, after hesitating and looking around a few times, the sheep turned and entered the pen and Mr Crossley banged the gate behind them.

As he did so, he turned to Sweep with a happy cry of "Good lad!" and the dog answered with a quick wag of his tail.

At that, Gyp, who had been standing very still, watching every move intently, raised his head and gave a single loud bark which echoed round the field.

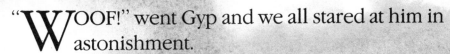

"WOOF!" went Gyp and we all stared at him in astonishment.

"Did you hear that?" gasped Mrs Wilkin.

"Well, I don't believe it!" her husband burst out, looking open-mouthed at his dog.

Gyp didn't seem to realise that he had done anything unusual. George Crossley came over with Sweep and the two dogs greeted each other happily. Mr Wilkin let Gyp off his lead and within seconds the two dogs were rolling around, chewing playfully at each other as they used to do as pups.

I suppose the Wilkins, as well as myself, had the feeling that this event might encourage Gyp to bark like any other dog, but it was not to be.

Six years later I was at the farm and went to the house to get some hot water. As Mrs Wilkin handed me the bucket, she looked down at Gyp who was basking in the sunshine outside the kitchen door.

"There you are, you funny fellow," she said to the dog.

I laughed. "Has he ever barked since that day?"

Mrs Wilkin shook her head. "No, he hasn't, not a sound. I waited a long time but I don't think he'll ever bark."

"Ah well, it's not important. But I'll never forget that afternoon at the trial," I said.

"Nor will I!" Mrs Wilkin looked at Gyp again, and she smiled as she remembered. "Poor old lad. Eight years old and only one woof!"

The Christmas Day Kitten

Illustrations by Ruth Brown

Christmas can never go by without my remembering a certain little cat. I first saw her when I called to see one of Mrs Pickering's much-loved Basset hounds.

I looked in some surprise at the furry creature moving quietly down the hall.

'I didn't know you had a cat,' I said to Mrs Pickering, who was a plumpish, pleasant-faced woman.

Mrs Pickering smiled. 'We haven't really. Debbie is a stray. She comes here two or three times a week and we give her some food. I don't know where she lives.'

'Do you ever get the feeling that she wants to stay with you?' I asked.

'No.' Mrs Pickering shook her head. 'She's a timid little thing. Just creeps in, has some food, then slips away. She doesn't seem to want to let me help her in any way.'

I looked at the little tabby cat again. 'But she isn't just having food today.'

'It's a funny thing, but every now and again she pops through into the sitting-room and sits by the fire for a few minutes. It's as though she was giving herself a treat.'

The little cat was sitting very upright on the thick rug which lay in front of the fireplace in which the coals glowed and flamed. The three Bassets were already lying there but they seemed used to Debbie because two of them sniffed her in a bored manner and the third merely cocked a sleepy eye at her before flopping back to sleep.

Debbie made no effort to curl up or wash herself or do anything other than gaze quietly ahead. This was obviously a special event in her life, a treat.

Then suddenly she turned and crept from the room
without a sound, and was gone.

'That's just the way it is with Debbie,' said Mrs Pickering,
laughing. 'She never stays more than ten minutes or so, then
she's off.'

I often visited the Pickering home and I always looked out
for the little cat. On one occasion I spotted her nibbling
daintily from a saucer at the kitchen door. As I watched, she
turned and almost floated on light footsteps into the hall,
then through into the sitting-room.

Debbie settled herself in the middle of the pile of Basset hounds in her usual way: upright, still, and gazing into the glowing fire.

This time, I tried to make friends with her but she leaned away as I stretched out my hand. However, I talked to her softly and I managed to stroke her cheek with one finger.

Then it was time for her to go and, once outside the house, she jumped up on to the stone wall and down the other side. The last I saw was the little tabby figure flitting away across the grassy field.

'I wonder where she goes?' I murmured.

'That's something we've never been able to find out,' said Mrs Pickering.

It was three months later that I next heard from Mrs Pickering – and it happened to be Christmas morning.

'I'm so sorry to bother you today of all days,' said Mrs Pickering apologetically.

'Don't worry at all,' I said. 'Which of the dogs needs attention?'

'It's not the dogs. It's … Debbie. She's come to the house and there's something very wrong. Please come quickly.'

I drove through the empty market square. The snow was thick on the road and on the roofs of the surrounding houses. The shops were closed but the pretty coloured lights of the Christmas trees winked in the windows.

Mrs Pickering's house was beautifully decorated with tinsel and holly, and the rich smell of turkey and sage and onion stuffing wafted from the kitchen. But she had a very worried look on her face as she led me through to the sitting-room.

Debbie was there, but she wasn't sitting upright in her usual position. She was lying quite still – and huddled close to her lay a tiny kitten.

I looked down in amazement. 'What have we got here?'
'It's the strangest thing,' Mrs Pickering replied. 'I haven't
seen her for several weeks and then she came in about two
hours ago, staggered into the kitchen, and she was carrying
the kitten in her mouth. She brought it in here and laid it on
the rug. Almost immediately I could see that she wasn't well.
Then she lay down like this and she hasn't moved since.

I knelt on the rug and passed my hand over Debbie's body which Mrs Pickering had placed on a piece of sheet. She was very, very thin and her coat was dirty. I knew that she didn't have long to live.

'Is she ill, Mr Herriot?' asked Mrs Pickering in a trembling voice.

'Yes … yes, I'm afraid so. But I don't think she is in any pain.'

Mrs Pickering looked at me and I saw there were tears in her eyes. Then she knelt beside Debbie and stroked the cat's head while the tears fell on the dirty fur.

'Oh, the poor little thing! I should have done more for her.'

I spoke gently. 'Nobody could have done more than you. Nobody could have been kinder. And see, she has brought her kitten to you, hasn't she?'

'Yes, you are right, she has.' Mrs Pickering reached out and lifted up the tiny, bedraggled kitten. 'Isn't it strange – Debbie knew she was dying so she brought her kitten here. And on Christmas Day.'

I bent down and put my hand on Debbie's heart. There was no beat. 'I'm afraid she has died.' I lifted the feather-light body, wrapped it in the piece of sheet and took it out to the car.

When I came back, Mrs Pickering was still stroking the kitten. The tears had dried, and she was bright-eyed as she looked at me.

'I've never had a cat before,' she said.

I smiled. 'Well, it looks as though you've got one now.'

And she certainly had. The kitten grew rapidly into a sleek, handsome and bouncy tabby cat and Mrs Pickering called him Buster. He wasn't timid like his little mother and he lived like a king – and with the ornate collar he always wore, looked like one too.

I watched him grow up with delight, but the occasion that always stays in my mind was the following Christmas Day, a year after his arrival.

I was on my way home after visiting a farmer with a sick cow, and I was looking forward to my Christmas dinner. Mrs Pickering was at her front door when I passed her house and I heard her call out, 'Merry Christmas, Mr Herriot! Come in and have a drink to warm you up.'

I had a little time to spare, so I stopped the car and went in. In the house there was all the festive cheer of last year and the same glorious whiff of sage and onion stuffing. But this year, there was no sorrow – there was Buster!

He was darting up to each of the Basset hounds in turn, ears pricked, eyes twinkling, dabbing a paw at them, and then streaking away.

Mrs Pickering laughed. 'Buster does tease them so. He gives them no peace.'

She was right. For a long time, the dogs had led a rather sedate life: gentle walks with their mistress, plenty of good food, and long snoring sessions on the rugs and armchairs. Then Buster arrived.

He was now dancing up to the youngest dog again, head on one side, asking him to play. When he started boxing with both paws, it was too much for the Basset who rolled over with the cat in a wrestling game.

'Come into the garden,' said Mrs Pickering. 'I want to show you something.'

She lifted a hard rubber ball from the sideboard and we went outside.

She threw the ball across the lawn and Buster bounded after it over the frosty grass, his tabby coat gleaming in the sun. He seized the ball in his mouth, brought it back to his mistress, dropped it at her feet, and waited. Mrs Pickering threw it and again Buster brought it back.

I gasped. A retriever-cat!

The Bassets looked on unimpressed. Nothing would ever make *them* chase a ball, but Buster did it again and again as though he would never tire of it.

Mrs Pickering turned to me. 'Have you ever seen anything like that?'

'No,' I replied. 'He is a most remarkable cat.'

We went back into the house where she held Buster close to her, laughing as the big cat purred loudly. Looking at him, so healthy and contented, I remembered his mother who had carried her tiny kitten to the only place of comfort and warmth that she had ever known.

Mrs Pickering was thinking the same thing because she turned to me and, although she was smiling, her eyes were thoughtful. 'Debbie would be pleased,' she said.

I nodded. 'Yes, she would. It was just a year ago today she brought him in, wasn't it?'

'That's right.' She hugged Buster again. 'The best Christmas present I've ever had.'

Bonny's Big Day

Illustrated by Ruth Brown

O ne sunny morning in early September, I drove to see
old John Skipton at Dale Close Farm since he had
telephoned to say that one of his carthorses was lame.

As I got out of the car, the untidily-dressed figure of the
farmer came through the kitchen door of Dale Close.

John always seemed to look like a scarecrow, and today was no different. He was wearing a tattered buttonless coat which was tied round his waist with string. His trousers were much too short and, as he hurried towards me, I could see that he was wearing socks of different colours – one was red, and the other was blue.

By working very hard when he was a young man, Mr Skipton had saved enough money to buy his own farm with its handsome stone house. He had never married and because he was always so busy looking after the sheep and cows on the hill, bringing in the harvest from the fields, and picking the apples in the orchard, he had been much too busy to worry about himself – which is why he was always dressed in such very old clothes.

'The horses are down by the river,' he said in his usual gruff manner. 'We'll have to go down there.' He seized a pitchfork and stabbed it into a big pile of hay which he then hoisted on to his shoulder. I pulled my large Gladstone bag from the car and set off behind him.

It was difficult to keep up with the farmer's brisk pace even though he must have been fifty years older than me. I was glad when we reached the bottom of the hill because the bag was heavy and I was getting rather hot.

I saw the two horses standing in the shallows of the pebbly river. They were nose to tail, and were rubbing their chins gently along each other's backs. Beyond them, a carpet of green turf ran up to a high sheltered ridge, while all around clumps of oak and beech blazed in the autumn sunshine.

'They're in a nice place, Mr Skipton,' I said.

'Aye, they can keep cool in the hot weather, and they've got the barn when the winter comes.'

At the sound of his voice, the two big horses came trotting up from the river – the grey one first, and the chestnut following a little more slowly, and limping slightly.

They were fine big carthorses, but I could see they were old from the sprinkling of white hairs on their faces. Despite their age, however, they pranced around old John, stamping their enormous feet, throwing their heads about and pushing the farmer's cap over his eyes with their muzzles.

'Get over, leave off!' he cried.

He pulled at the grey horse's forelock. 'This is Bonny, she's well over twenty years old.' Then he ran his hand down the front leg of the chestnut. 'And this is Dolly. She's nearly thirty now, and not one day's sickness until now.'

'When did they last do any work?' I asked.

'Oh, about twelve years ago, I reckon,' the farmer replied.

I stared at him in amazement. 'Twelve years? Have they been down here all that time?'

'Aye, just playing about down here. They've earned their retirement.'

For a few seconds he stood silent, shoulders hunched, hands deep in the pockets of his tattered coat.

'They worked very hard when I had to struggle to get this farm going,' he murmured, and I knew he was thinking of the long years those horses had pulled the plough, drawn the hay and harvest wagons, and had done all the hard work which the tractors now do.

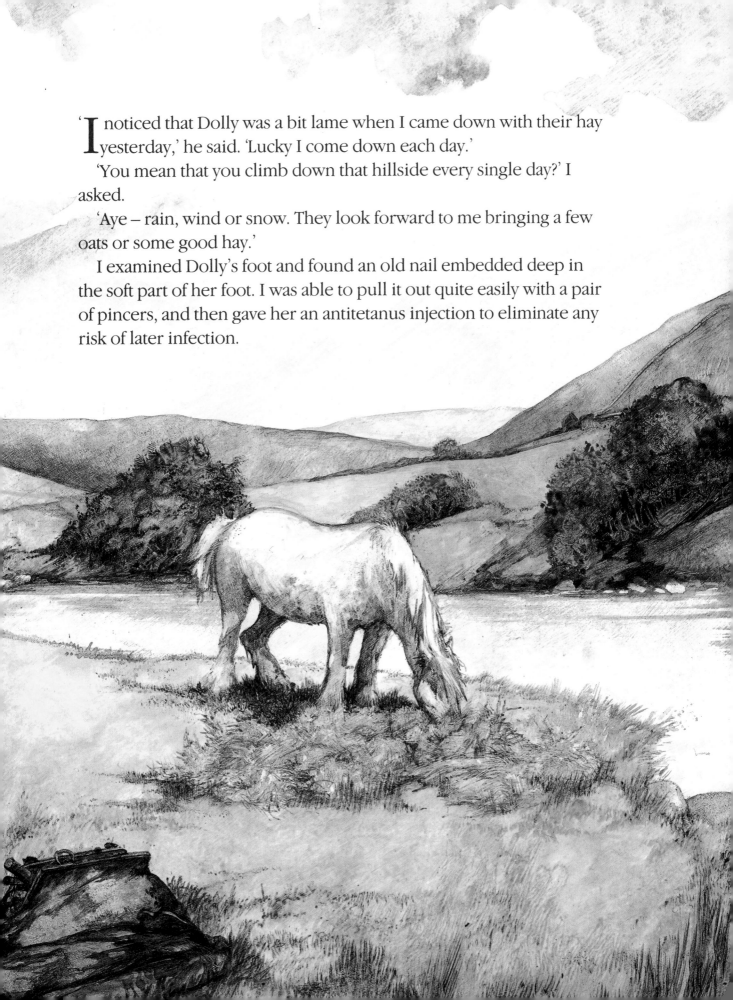

'I noticed that Dolly was a bit lame when I came down with their hay yesterday,' he said. 'Lucky I come down each day.'

'You mean that you climb down that hillside every single day?' I asked.

'Aye – rain, wind or snow. They look forward to me bringing a few oats or some good hay.'

I examined Dolly's foot and found an old nail embedded deep in the soft part of her foot. I was able to pull it out quite easily with a pair of pincers, and then gave her an antitetanus injection to eliminate any risk of later infection.

Climbing back up the hill, I couldn't help thinking how wonderful it was that old John had made the long journey to see the horses in all weathers, every day for twelve years. He certainly loved those great animals.

A thought struck me, and I turned to him. 'You know, Mr Skipton, it's the Darrowby Show next Saturday. You should enter the mares in the Family Pets Class. I know they are asking for unusual entries this year. Perhaps you should only take Bonny since Dolly's foot will be a bit sore for a few days.'

The farmer frowned. 'What on earth are you talking about?'

'Go on,' I said. 'Take Bonny to the show! Those horses are your pets, aren't they?'

'Pets!' he snorted. 'You couldn't call one of those great big clod-hoppers a pet. I've never heard anything so silly.'

When he got back to the farmyard, he thanked me gruffly, gave me a nod and disappeared into his house.

The following Saturday, it was my duty to attend Darrowby Show as the vet-in-charge. I had spent a pleasant time strolling around the showground, looking at the pens of cattle and sheep, the children's ponies, the massive bulls, and the sheepdog trials in the neighbouring fields.

Then over the loudspeaker came the following announcement: 'Would the entrants for the Family Pets Class please take their places in the ring.'

I was always interested in this event, so I walked over and stood by
the Secretary who was sitting at a table near the edge of the ring. He
was Darrowby's local bank manager, a prim little man with rimless
spectacles and a pork pie hat. I could see that he was pleased at the
number of entrants now filing into the ring.

He looked at me and beamed. 'They have certainly taken me at my
word when I asked for unusual entries this year.'

The parade was led by a fine white nanny goat which was followed
by a pink piglet. Apart from numerous cats and dogs of all shapes
and sizes, there was a goldfish in its bowl, and at least five rabbits.
There was a parrot on a perch, and some budgies having an outing in
their cage. Then to an excited buzz of conversation, a man walked
into the ring with a hooded falcon on his wrist.

'Splendid, splendid!' cried Mr Secretary – but then his mouth fell
open and everyone stopped talking as a most unexpected sight
appeared.

Old John Skipton came striding into the ring, and he was leading Bonny – but it was a quite different man and horse than I had seen a few days before.

John still wore the same old tattered coat tied with string, but today I noticed that both his socks were the same colour and on his head, perched right in the centre, was an ancient bowler hat.

It made him look almost smart, but not as smart as Bonny. She was dressed in the full show regalia of an old-fashioned carthorse. Her hooves were polished and oiled, the long feathery hair on her lower limbs had been washed and fluffed out; her mane, tail and forelock had been plaited with green and yellow ribbons, and her coat had been groomed until it shone in the sunshine. She was wearing part of the harness from her working days and it, too, had been polished, and little bells hung from the collar.

It quite took my breath away to look at her.

'Mr Skipton, Mr Skipton! You can't bring that great thing in here. This is the class for Family Pets!' cried Mr Secretary leaping up from his chair.

'Bonny *is* my pet,' responded the farmer. 'She's part of my family. Just like that old goat over there.'

'Well, I disagree,' said Mr Secretary, waving his arms. 'You must take her out of the ring, and go home.'

Old John Skipton put on a fierce face and glared at the man. 'Bonny *is* my pet,' he repeated. 'Just ask Mr Herriot.'

I shrugged my shoulders. 'Perfectly true. This mare hasn't worked for over twelve years and is kept entirely for Mr Skipton's pleasure. I'd certainly call Bonny a pet.'

'But…but…' spluttered Mr Secretary. Then he sat down suddenly on his chair, and sighed, 'Oh, very well then, go and get into line.'

So John turned and led Bonny to a place right in the middle of the other competitors. On one side of them was the little pink piglet, and on the other side a tortoise. It was a most curious sight.

The task of judging the pets had been given to the district nurse who was very sensibly dressed in her official uniform to give her an air of authority. Judging this class was always difficult, and when she looked along the line and kept seeing the great horse, she knew it was going to be very difficult indeed.

She looked carefully at every competitor, but her eyes always came back to Bonny. All the rabbits were very sweet, the falcon was impressive, the dogs were charming, and the piglet was cute – but Bonny was *MAGNIFICENT!*

'First prize to Mr Skipton and Bonny,' she announced and everyone cheered.

As the rosette was presented, a man came to take a photograph for the local newspaper. It looked as though the great horse knew all about her prize as she posed there, dignified and beautiful. John too stood very erect and proud – but, unfortunately, every time the photographer clicked the camera, Bonny pushed the bowler hat over the farmer's eyes.

It was the mare's way of showing her love, but I couldn't help wondering how the picture would come out.

After the show, I went back to Dale Close to help John 'undress' Bonny – and I went with them down the hill to the field by the river.

As we approached, Dolly came trotting up from the river, whinnying with pleasure to see her friend and companion again.

'Her foot is quite healed now,' I said, noting the horse's even stride.

In the gentle evening light we watched the two old horses hurry towards each other. Then for a long time, they stood rubbing their faces together.

'Look at that,' said old John with one of his rare smiles. 'Bonny is telling Dolly all about her big day!'

Bonny takes first prize in the Family Pets class
(The Darrowby and Houlton Times)

Blossom
Comes Home

Illustrated by Ruth Brown

I arrived at Mr Dakin's farm just outside Darrowby on a warm
April morning. The green hillside ran down to the river, and
the spring sunshine danced on the water. The birds were singing
and lambs played on the flower-strewn pastures.

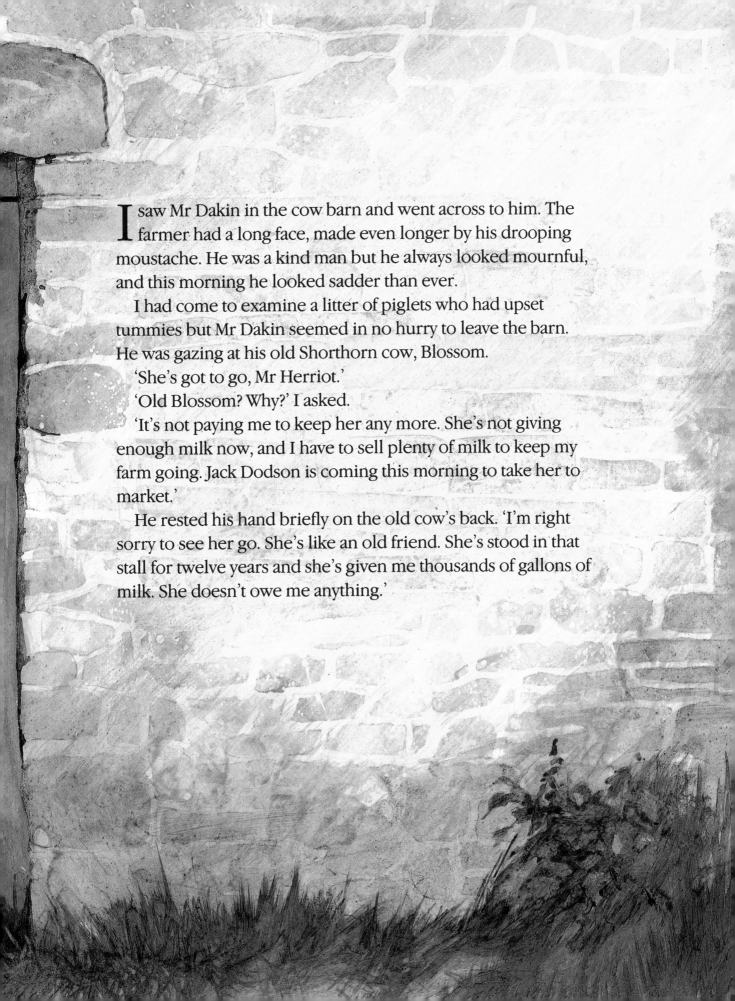

I saw Mr Dakin in the cow barn and went across to him. The farmer had a long face, made even longer by his drooping moustache. He was a kind man but he always looked mournful, and this morning he looked sadder than ever.

I had come to examine a litter of piglets who had upset tummies but Mr Dakin seemed in no hurry to leave the barn. He was gazing at his old Shorthorn cow, Blossom.

'She's got to go, Mr Herriot.'

'Old Blossom? Why?' I asked.

'It's not paying me to keep her any more. She's not giving enough milk now, and I have to sell plenty of milk to keep my farm going. Jack Dodson is coming this morning to take her to market.'

He rested his hand briefly on the old cow's back. 'I'm right sorry to see her go. She's like an old friend. She's stood in that stall for twelve years and she's given me thousands of gallons of milk. She doesn't owe me anything.'

BLOSSOM

There were only six cows in the old cobbled barn with its low roof and wooden partitions, and they all had names. You don't find cows with names any more, and there aren't many farmers like Mr Dakin who somehow scratch a living from a herd of six milking cows and a few calves, pigs and hens.

As if she knew she were the topic of conversation, Blossom turned her head and looked at him. She was certainly very ancient: her pelvic bones jutted out from her skinny body and her udder drooped almost to the ground. But there was something appealing in the friendliness of the eyes and the patient expression on her face.

Mr Dakin had fallen silent as he looked fondly at his cow. I was about to suggest that we might see the piglets when I heard a clattering of boots in the yard and Jack Dodson, the cattle-drover, hurried into the barn.

'Now then, Mr Dakin,' he cried. 'It's easy to see which one you want me to take. It's that skinny old thing over there.'

He pointed to Blossom and, in truth, the unkind description seemed to fit the bony creature standing among her sleek neighbours.

The farmer didn't reply for a moment, then he went between the cows and gently rubbed Blossom's forehead. 'Aye, this is the one, Jack.' Then he undid the chain round her neck. 'Off you go, old lass,' he murmured, and the cow turned and made her way placidly from the stall.

'Come along, come along!' shouted Jack Dodson, prodding the cow's rump.

'Don't hit her!' barked Mr Dakin.

Mr Dodson looked at him in surprise. 'I never hit 'em, you know that. Just help 'em along, like.'

'All right,' Mr Dakin replied. 'But you won't need your stick for this one. She'll go wherever you want, always has done.'

Blossom proved him right and ambled across the yard. She turned up the track to join a group of fat bullocks and cows standing on the road high above. A boy and a dog circled them, keeping them together.

The farmer and I stood watching as Blossom made her way unhurriedly up the hill, Jack Dodson following behind her. As the path wound behind an old grey barn, man and beast disappeared – but Mr Dakin still gazed after them, listening to the clip-clop of the hooves on the hard ground.

When the sound had died away, he turned to me quickly. 'Right, Mr Herriot, we'll get on with seeing those little pigs.'

There were twelve squealing piglets in the sty with their mother. The farmer gently picked each one up and held it while I gave it an injection which would make it better. This took me about fifteen minutes and I tried to pass the time by talking about the weather, cricket matches and other things, but Mr Dakin replied only with a series of grunts. I could see that he was still sad about Blossom.

I, too, was thinking about the old cow as I drove away from the farm, up the track and on to the road above. On my way home, I had to pass through the nearby village of Briston, and as I arrived, I saw the herd of cattle at the far end of the street. Mr Dodson was making another collection, and the boy was chatting to some friends by the roadside. I could see Blossom at the rear of the group, with her head turned, looking back.

Briston was where Mrs Pickering lived with her three Basset hounds and Buster, the cat who was once her Christmas Day kitten. One of the dogs had broken his leg a month before and I had to remove the plaster cast this morning.

I lifted the dog on to the table and while I was cutting away the plaster, Buster kept frisking around, pawing playfully at my hand as the solemn-faced Bassets looked on disapprovingly.

After I had taken off the cast, I could see that the leg had set very well. 'He'll be fine now, Mrs Pickering,' I said.

Just then, I saw a single unattended cow trot past the window. This was unusual because cows always have somebody in charge and, anyway, there was something familiar about this one. I hurried to the window and looked out. It was Blossom!

'Please excuse me,' I said to Mrs Pickering. I packed my bag quickly, and rushed out to my car.

B lossom was moving down the village street at a good pace, her eyes fixed steadily ahead as though she were going somewhere important. What on earth had happened? She should have been at Darrowby market by now. People in the street were staring at her and the postman nearly fell off his bike as she pushed past him. Then she disappeared round the corner and out of sight.

I had to turn the car, and then I drove after her at top speed – but when I rounded the corner, there was no sign of her, and the road that stretched ahead of me was empty. She had vanished – but where had she gone?

One thing was certain. I had to go back to Mr Dakin's farm and tell him that Blossom had broken away and was loose in the countryside.

I urged my little car as fast as I could and when I reached the farm, I met Mr Dakin carrying a sack of grain across the yard.

He looked at me in surprise 'Hello, Mr Herriot. Have you forgotten something?'

I was about to blurt out my story when he raised his head suddenly, and listened. 'What's that?' he said.

From somewhere on the hillside above us, I could hear the clip-clop of hooves. As we stood in the yard and listened, a cow rounded a rocky outcrop and came towards us. It was Blossom, moving at a brisk trot, great udder swinging, eyes fixed purposefully on the barn door.

'What on earth...' burst out Mr Dakin, but the old cow
brushed past us and marched without hesitation into the
stall she had occupied for the past twelve years. She sniffed
enquiringly at the empty hay rack and looked round at her
astonished owner.

Mr Dakin stared back at her. The eyes in the weathered face
were watery, and he began to pull thoughtfully at his long
moustache.

The silence was broken by the sound of heavy boots on the cobbles of the yard, and Jack Dodson panted his way through the door.

'Oh, there you are, you old scallywag!' he gasped. 'I'm right sorry, Mr Dakin. I left that lad in charge for a few minutes and he let her escape.' Then he moved towards Blossom. 'Come on, lass, let's be having you out of there.'

But he halted as Mr Dakin held an arm in front of him.

There was a long silence as Dodson looked in surprise at the farmer who continued to gaze at the cow. There was a quiet dignity about the old animal as she stood there against the crumbling timbers of the partition, her eyes patient and undemanding.

Then, still without speaking, Mr Dakin moved unhurriedly between the cows and the faint click of metal sounded as he fastened the chain around Blossom's neck. Next he strolled to the end of the barn and returned with a forkful of hay which he tossed expertly into the wooden rack.

This was what Blossom was waiting for. She snatched a mouthful and began to chew with quiet satisfaction.

'What's going on?' cried Jack Dodson in bewilderment. 'I'll be late for market.'

'I'm sorry I've wasted your time, Jack,' the farmer replied slowly, 'but you'll have to go without her.'

'Without her... but...?' spluttered Mr Dodson.

'Aye, you'll think I'm daft, but that's how it is. The old lass has come home and she's staying home.'

Mr Dodson shook his head, and left to get back to the market.

'Mr Herriot,' he said, 'do you ever feel that sometimes when unexpected things happen, they were meant to, and that it works out for the best in the end?'

'Yes,' I said, 'I often think that.'

'Well, that's how I felt when Blossom came back down the hill.' He reached out and scratched the old cow's back. 'She's always been my favourite and I'm glad she's back.'

I was still puzzled. 'But I can't understand how she got here. Why didn't I see her on the road? Where did she disappear to?'

A smile spread slowly across Mr Dakin's face, and he pulled again at his long moustache. 'Oh, there's another way to the farm. A little path which starts near the village.'

'And Blossom knows that path?'

'Oh aye, the old girl knows everything about this place.'

I looked at the six cows in a row. 'Didn't you say that you couldn't afford to keep her?' I asked, worried.

'That's right, but I've had an idea,' the farmer replied. 'I can put two or three calves on to her instead of milking her. The old stable across the yard is empty and she can live in there quite happily.'

'What a wonderful idea, Mr Dakin. She'll be very comfortable there and she'd suckle three calves easily. She would probably pay her way.'

'Well, I'm not worried about that,' said the farmer smiling. 'After all these years, she doesn't owe me anything. The important thing is that Blossom has come home.'

THE MARKET SQUARE DOG

Illustrated by Ruth Brown

On market days when the farmers around Darrowby brought their goods to the little town to sell, I used to take a walk across the cobbled square to meet the farmers who gathered there to chat. One of the farmers was telling me about his sick cow when we saw the little dog among the market stalls. The thing that made us notice the dog was that he was sitting up, begging, in front of the stall selling cakes and biscuits.

'Look at that little chap,' the farmer said. 'I wonder where he's come from?'

As he spoke, the stallholder threw him a bun which the dog devoured eagerly, but when the man came round and stretched out a hand the little animal trotted away. He stopped, however, at another stall which sold eggs, butter, cheese and scones. Without hesitation, he sat up again in the begging position, rock steady, paws dangling, head pointing expectantly.

I nudged my companion. 'There he goes again.
I always think a dog looks very appealing sitting up like that.'
The farmer nodded. 'Yes, he's a bonny little thing, isn't he?
What breed would you call him?'
'A cross, I'd say. He's like a small sheepdog, but there's a
touch of something else – maybe terrier.'

It wasn't long before the dog was munching a biscuit, and this time I walked over to him, and as I drew near I spoke gently. 'Here, boy,' I said, squatting down in front of him. 'Come on, let's have a look at you.'

He turned to face me, and for a moment two friendly brown eyes gazed at me from a wonderfully attractive face. The fringed tail waved in response to my words, but as I moved nearer he turned and trotted away among the market-day crowd until he was lost to sight.

I was standing there, trying to see where he had gone, when a
young policeman came up to me.

'I've been watching that wee dog begging among the stalls all
morning,' he said, 'but, like you, I haven't been able to get near him.'

'Yes, it's strange. You can see he's friendly, but he's also afraid.
I wonder who owns him.'

'I reckon he's a stray, Mr Herriot. I'm interested in dogs myself and I fancy I know just about all of them around here. But this one is a stranger to me.'

I nodded. 'I'm sure you're right. Anything could have happened to him. He could have been ill-treated by somebody and run away, or he could have been dumped from a car.'

'Yes,' the policeman replied, 'there are some cruel people about. I don't know how anybody can leave a helpless animal to fend for itself like that. I've had a few tries at catching him, but it's no good.'

The memory stayed with me for the rest of the day. It is our duty to look after the animals who depend on us and it worried me to think of the little creature wandering about in a strange place, sitting up and asking for help in the only way he knew.

Market day is on a Monday and on the Friday of that week my wife Helen and I had a treat planned for ourselves; we were going to the races in Brawton. Helen was making up a picnic basket with home-made ham-and-egg-pie, chicken sandwiches and a chocolate cake. I was wearing my best suit and I couldn't help feeling very smart because country vets have to work mostly in the fields and cowsheds and I hardly ever got dressed up. Helen, too, had put on her best dress and a fancy hat I had never seen before. As a vet's wife, she too had to work very hard and we weren't able to go out together very often.

We were just about to leave the house when the doorbell rang. It was the young policeman I had been talking to on market day.

'I've got that dog, Mr Herriot,' he said. 'You know – the one that was begging in the market square.'

'Oh good,' I replied, 'so you managed to catch him at last.'

The policeman paused. 'No, not really. One of our men found him lying by the roadside about a mile out of town and brought him in. I'm afraid he's been knocked down. We've got him here in the car.'

I went out and looked into the car. The little dog was lying very still on the back seat, but when I stroked the dark coat his tail stirred briefly.

'He can still manage a wag, anyway,' I said.

The policeman nodded. 'Yes, there's no doubt he's a good-natured wee thing.'

I tried to examine him as much as possible without touching because I didn't want to hurt him, but I could see that he had cuts all over his body and one hind leg lay in such a way that I knew it must be broken. When I gently lifted his head, I saw that one eyelid was badly torn so that the eye was completely closed. But the other soft brown eye looked at me trustingly.

'Can you do anything for him, Mr Herriot?' asked the policeman. 'Can you save him?'

'I'll do my best,' I replied.

I carried the little animal into the surgery and laid him on the table.

'There's an hour or two's work here, Helen,' I said to my wife. 'I'm very sorry, but we won't be able to go to the races.'

'Never mind,' she replied. 'We must do what we can for this fellow.'

Rather sadly she took off her fancy hat and I took off my good jacket. Dressed in our white coats we began to work.

Helen was used to helping me and she gave the anaesthetic, then I set the broken leg in plaster and stitched up the wounds. The worst thing was the eye because even after I had stitched the eyelid it was still bruised and tightly closed and I was worried that he might lose the sight in that eye.

By the time we had finished, it was too late to go out anywhere, but Helen was quite cheerful. 'We can still have our picnic,' she said.

We carried the sleeping dog out to the garden and laid him
on a mat on the lawn so that we could watch him as he
came round from the anaesthetic.

Out there in the old high-walled garden the sun shone down
on the flowers and the apple trees. Helen put on her fancy hat
again and I put my smart jacket back on and as we sat there,
enjoying the good things from the picnic basket, we felt that we
were still having a day out. But Helen kept glancing anxiously at
the little dog and I knew she was thinking the same thing as I
was. Would he be all right after all that we had done for him
and, even then, what was going to happen to him?
Would his owners ever come to claim him, because
if they didn't, he had nobody in the world to
look after him.

Since he had been found by the police, he was officially classified as a stray and had to go into the kennels at the police station. When I visited him there two days later, he greeted me excitedly, balancing well on his plastered leg, his tail swishing. All his fear seemed to have gone. I was delighted to see that the injured eye was now fully open, and the swelling down.

The young policeman was as pleased as I was. 'Look at that!' he exclaimed. 'He's nearly as good as new again.'

'Yes,' I said, 'he's done wonderfully well.' I hesitated for a moment. 'Has anybody enquired about him?'

He shook his head. 'Nothing yet, but we'll keep hoping, and in the meantime we'll take good care of him here.'

I visited the kennels often, and each time the shaggy little creature jumped up to greet me, laughing into my face, mouth open, eyes shining. But nobody seemed to want him.

After a few more days it was clear that no owner was going to claim him, and my only hope was that somebody else would take him and give him a home.

There were other stray dogs in the kennels, and on one visit I saw a farmer calling to collect his wandering sheepdog.

Then a family was overjoyed at being reunited with their handsome golden retriever.

Finally a little old lady came in and tearfully gathered her tiny Yorkshire terrier into her arms. But nobody came for my little patient.

Various strangers came too, looking for a pet, but nobody seemed to be interested in him. Maybe it was because he was only a mongrel and the people who visited the kennels wanted a more elegant dog – yet I knew that he would make a perfect pet for anybody.

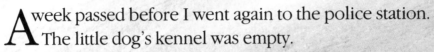

A week passed before I went again to the police station. The little dog's kennel was empty.

'What's happened?' I asked the policeman. 'Has somebody taken him?'

The policeman looked very grave. 'No,' he replied, 'I'm afraid he's been arrested.'

'Arrested?' I said in astonishment. 'What do you mean?'

'Well,' he said, 'it seems that it's against the law for a dog to go begging in the market square so he has been taken into police custody.'

I was bewildered. 'What are you talking about? A dog can't be arrested.'

The policeman, still very solemn, shrugged his shoulders. 'This dog was.'

'I still don't know what this is all about,' I said. 'Where is he now?'

'I'll take you to him,' the policeman replied.

We left the police station and walked a short way along the road to a pretty cottage.

We went inside and there, in the sitting-room, curled up in a big new doggy bed was my little friend. Two small girls were sitting by his side, stroking his coat.

The policeman threw back his head and laughed. 'I've just been kidding you, Mr Herriot. This is my house and I've taken him as a pet for my two daughters. They've been wanting a dog for some time and I've got so fond of this wee chap that I thought he'd be just right for them.'

A wave of relief swept over me. 'Well, that's wonderful,' I said and I looked at his kind face gratefully. 'What's your name?' I asked.

'Phelps,' he replied. 'PC Phelps. And they call me Funny Phelps at the police station because I like playing jokes on people.'

'Well, you certainly took me in,' I said. 'Arrested indeed!'

He laughed again. 'Well, you've got to admit he's in the hands of the law now!'

I laughed too. I didn't mind having the joke played on me because, funny Phelps or not, he was obviously a nice Phelps and would be a kind master for my doggy friend.

It was a happy day when I took the plaster off the little dog's leg and found that the break had healed perfectly. All the nasty cuts had healed, too, and when I lifted him down from the table, the small girls held up a beautiful new red collar with a lead to match. Their new pet liked the look of them because he sat up in that position I remembered so well, his paws dangling, his face looking up eagerly. The begging dog had found a home at last.

Oscar,
Cat-About-Town

Illustrations by Ruth Brown

I looked at the stray cat which a kind little girl had brought to my examining room. He was very pretty with stripes of auburn, gold and grey, but he looked terribly thin and ill.

The little girl said that nobody knew where the cat had come from, so she left him with me.

With my wife Helen by my side I examined him thoroughly and found that he was suffering from starvation. But the strange thing was that he purred loudly all the time.

'He's so weak that he can hardly stand, but he's purring,' I said. 'You can see he's a good-natured cat.'

For a few days Helen gave him beef broth and milk to make him strong and when he walked into the kitchen to eat some of Sam's dinner of meat and biscuits, we knew he was well again.

'We shall call him Oscar,' Helen said.

'You mean you want to keep him?'

'Yes, he's a lovely, friendly cat, and so pretty, and since we don't know who owns him, he must stay with us. He and Sam seem to get along so well.' Oscar purred his approval and his big purr became part of our lives.

Oscar had been with us for several weeks when I came home and found Helen looking very worried. 'It's Oscar. He's gone!' she said.

'What do you mean?'

'I think he's run away.'

I became worried too because I knew he had run away from somewhere before we found him and it made me sad to think that we might be going to lose our cat after we had grown so fond of him.

In the darkness, Helen and I searched all over the garden and the lane behind the house. Then, although it had begun to rain heavily, we began to explore the streets and side-alleys of the little town of Darrowby. After two hours we could not find him and Helen had tears in her eyes.

'I think we'd better go home, Jim,' she said. 'He's gone, I know he has.'

On our way home, we passed the brightly-lit window of the Women's Institute Hall. I stopped suddenly. 'I think I can see Oscar in there!' I cried. We both peered in through the window and to our delight we could see our cat among the ladies.

We ran inside. There was a hat-making competition in progress. Various ladies were lined up, wearing some very original and pretty hats. Oscar was walking along with the judge, listening to her comments and examining each hat as though he himself were an expert. Sometimes he jumped up in the air to have a closer look.

When we were able to reach Oscar he was delighted to see us and purred and rubbed round our legs. One of the ladies said that he had been there for the whole evening and had seemed to enjoy himself thoroughly.

It was lovely to have him back – but one afternoon a
week later, he disappeared again. Helen and I looked
everywhere and again we were just giving up hope when
we heard two women speaking as they came out of
Darrowby's Town Hall.

'Did you see that funny cat in there?' one of them said,
laughing. 'I've never seen one like him.'

Helen and I looked at each other, then hurried into the
hall where a rummage was taking place. And there was
Oscar right in the thick of things.

He was stepping daintily along the display tables, inspecting the old shoes, books, pictures, ornaments, crockery, and he looked really happy. Now and then he cocked his head on one side when something caught his fancy. Once more it was clear that he was enjoying every moment and we didn't want to disturb him, but the sale was soon over and he greeted us with joy.

When he went missing again on the following Saturday
we were not so worried because we knew he would
be at some gathering.

'Darrowby School is playing Wickley School at soccer
today,' Helen said.

We rushed round to the soccer field and, as we expected,
Oscar was there among the spectators, running along the
line, following the ball, jumping up and down at the
cheering. We let him enjoy himself for a while before
bringing him home, and then we had a chat by the fireside.

'Now we know,' said Helen.

I nodded. 'Yes, when he disappears, he isn't running away at all. He's just visiting. He likes getting around, he loves people, especially in groups, and he's interested in what they do. He's a natural mixer.'

Helen looked down at our cat. 'Of course, that's it . . . he's a socialite!'

'Exactly, a high-stepper!'

'A swinger!'

'A cat-about-town!'

We both laughed, not only because it was a funny idea but because we were relieved that Oscar wasn't going to run away after all. Oscar seemed to be laughing, too, as he looked up at us, adding his loud, throbbing purr to the merriment.

We were all happy and everything seemed to be perfect – but a few days later we received an unexpected blow.

I was finishing my office hours. I looked round the door of the waiting room and saw only a man and two little red-headed boys. Helen came in and began to tidy the magazines on the table.

The man had the rough, weathered face of a farmer and he twirled a cloth cap nervously in his hands.

'Mr Herriot,' he said, 'my name is Sep Gibbons and I think you've got my cat.'

'What makes you think that?' I asked in surprise.

'Well, when we moved from Darrowby to Wickley, the cat went missing. We thought he might be trying to find his way back to his old home. We hunted everywhere, but we couldn't find him. My boys were broken-hearted. They loved that cat.'

'But why do you think we've got him?'

'Well, my boys were playing soccer here last week and they are sure they spotted him watching the game. He always liked to be with people, go to meetings and social events. So I just had to come and find out.'

'This cat you lost,' I asked, 'what did he look like?'

'Sort of tabby but with gingery stripes. He was very handsome.'

My heart thumped.

That sounded very like Oscar.

I could see that Helen was worried, too. 'Just a moment,' she said. 'Oscar's in the kitchen. I'll bring him through.'

When she returned with the cat in her arms, the little boys called out, 'Tiger! Oh, Tiger, Tiger!'

'That's our cat, all right,' said Mr Gibbons. 'And doesn't he look well! The boys called him Tiger because of his gingery stripes.'

He looked at the two boys flopped happily on the floor as Oscar, purring loudly with delight, rolled around them. 'The boys used to play with him like that for hours. They cried a lot when we lost him.'

'Well, Mr Gibbons,' said Helen with a catch in her voice, 'you'd better take him. He was your cat first, and you searched for him so hard, and I can see that the boys love him.'

'Well, that's very kind of you. Please come and see him whenever you like. Wickley is only twenty miles away.' He picked up Oscar and left.

We missed Oscar terribly, but we knew we had done the right thing. He really belonged to the Gibbons family who loved him and would be kind to him.

One afternoon we were out shopping in the nearby town, and I looked at my watch. 'It's only five o'clock. Why don't we go and see Oscar at Wickley, it's not far from here.'

The Gibbons' cottage was at the far end of Wickley village and when Mrs Gibbons opened the door to us she didn't know who we were, but when she heard the name Herriot, she was delighted to see us.

'Come in and have a cup of tea,' she said.

We went inside and were greeted by Sep and the boys. As Mrs Gibbons busied herself with the kettle, we looked eagerly around the room for Oscar and within a few moments he trotted in. He took one look at Helen, then jumped onto her lap, and rubbed his face against her hand.

'He knows me, he knows me!' Helen cried in delight.

'Yes,' Sep said. 'You were kind to him and he'll never forget you, and we won't either.'

I tickled the cat's cheek as he lay curled happily on Helen's lap. However, after about half an hour he gave her a final rub and purr, then jumped down and trotted from the room into the back garden.

Mrs Gibbons laughed. 'He still goes visiting. Let's see, Thursday, isn't it? That's when he goes to the brass band practice at the village hall. It's just next door and he slips through a hole in the hedge.'

'Oh, let's go and see him!' Helen said.

'We'll pop round there when we've finished our tea,' said Mrs Gibbons.

In the village hall, we all stood in a row and watched
Oscar moving among the band players, jumping in delight
at each boom from the drum, creeping close to the slide of
the trombone which seemed to fascinate him.

'There's Oscar!' I said. 'There's Tiger!' said one of the boys,
and we all laughed.

'It doesn't matter what we call him,' said Sep. 'He belongs
to all of us now.'

SMUDGE, THE LITTLE LOST LAMB

Illustrated by Ruth Brown

H arry had got up very early in the morning to help his father with the lambs. He had enjoyed holding the ewe and then rubbing down the newborn lambs with straw to dry them. He liked all the animals on the farm, and often helped his father with the cows, calves and pigs, but spring was his favorite time, when the lambs were born.

'They are grand, strong lambs,' said Farmer Cobb, looking down at the twin lambs who were standing in the pen by their mother. 'It was very good of you to get up early to help me, Harry. Would you like to have these two lambs for yourself?'

'Oh, yes please, Dad,' said Harry.

'All right then, they're yours. You must keep an eye on them every day. What are you going to call them?'

Harry thought for a moment. 'That one has got a funny white mark on his nose. I'll call him Smudge - and his sister can be Smartie.'

'Those are good names. Now it's time you got ready for school, so off you go.'

A few days later, Harry was with his father when all the ewes and lambs were turned out into the field. Farmer Cobb looked at the flock spreading out across the wide expanse of grass. There were about a hundred ewes, most of them with twin lambs but some with just one and a few with three. The field had walls on three sides, but where it met the lane there were posts and wire.

'I hope I've fastened that wire down tightly enough,' he said.

'Some of these Swaledale lambs will try to get underneath it. In fact, some aren't happy until they've found a way out of the field.'

Farmer Cobb didn't know it at the time, but Smudge was one of those lambs.

For three weeks the flock grazed in the spring sunshine, the ewes cropping the young grass and the lambs playing happily and enjoying their mothers' milk. One of the lambs' favorite games was to collect in little groups and dash up and down by the side of a wall. Harry used to laugh when he saw them racing along, leaping joyfully in the air.

However, among the happy throng there was one lamb who wasn't content and that was Smudge. He enjoyed the games well enough, but every day he had a growing urge to see what was outside the field. He was getting very tired of seeing only the walls and the stretch of wire. In fact, at the age of three weeks, Smudge was bored.

He longed to escape and see what the world was like outside, and surely, he thought, there was some way he could get under that wire. Each day he worked his way along, nosing at where the wire met the grass, but Farmer Cobb had done his job well. Smudge was about to give up hope when, one morning, he found a tiny gap. He was able to get his nose through; then, as he thrust and pushed, he got his neck, then all his body, through and with a final wriggle he found himself on the other side.

Oh, the sensation of freedom was wonderful as he looked up and down the pretty little country road. He could go wherever he pleased, the whole world was his to explore, and he felt quite sorry for all his friends still imprisoned in the field. Oh, how clever he had been, he thought, as he puffed out his little chest and strutted along to the bend in the lane.

He could see for miles down a long valley. There were cattle and Dales ponies grazing on the green slopes which ran down to a pebbly river spanned by a fine stone bridge with three arches.

He gazed wonderingly at this new sight for some time;
then he nibbled at the long grass by the road before running
and skipping gleefully in the other direction. He was thrilled
to be able to see the battlements of a ruined castle towering
over the roofs of the village a mile away.

This was such fun! He leaped high in the air for sheer joy.
He felt so important: none of the other lambs knew anything
of this fascinating world outside the field. As he trotted
around, picking at the grass, looking eagerly around him, he
knew that this was what he had always wanted.

However, after about an hour of exploration, Smudge glanced through the wire and could see his sister Smartie suckling her mother, her tail wagging furiously. Suddenly he realised that he was hungry. He decided he would slip back and have some of that lovely milk before coming out again later. After all, he could do just as he liked now.

He pushed his nose at the wire. But where was the gap? It wasn't where he thought it should be. As he worked his way along without finding an opening, his heart beat faster, and when he tried again and again without success he began to feel really frightened and baa'd loudly for his mother. She replied to his shrill call with a deep baa but she couldn't do anything to help. Soon there was a deafening chorus of Smudge's high-pitched baa and his mother's deep one.

All he wanted now was to get back into the field, but his fear turned to terror as a huge dog came along the lane and rushed at him, barking and snarling.

S mudge ran away as fast as he could, and just as the dog was about to catch him, he dived between the bars of a gate into a field on the other side of the lane.

He was safe from the dog who couldn't get through, but Smudge found himself looking up into the face of an enormous bull. He had never seen such a monster and when the bull bent down until the shining bronze ring in his nose almost touched the lamb's face, Smudge fled at even greater speed.

He ran and ran and ran over the pasture until he came to a gate which opened on to the main road. He looked back. The bull was still lumbering after him, probably just out of curiosity, but Smudge, in his panic, shot straight across the road between the speeding cars and a bus whose startled passengers stared out at him.

He soon found himself on the outskirts of a village where he hid in a shed. He stayed there for ages, too frightened to move, but when it was dark he ventured out into a strange, unfamiliar world. Where was he? Where was his field with his mother and Smartie; how he longed for them. As he walked slowly along the road he felt hungrier than ever and was now exceedingly tired. He was so weak he could hardly do more than stagger from side to side.

Then, in the darkness, a bitter wind sprang up, blowing little flakes of snow into his face. Within a few minutes the kind of blizzard which sometimes appears without warning in the Yorkshire spring was raging around him.

S mudge's faltering steps took him to a cottage, just visible
in the darkness, and he huddled against the gate. He
tried to find some protection from the driving snow, but
there was no shelter and he did not have the strength to
walk any further. He felt very, very tired and very, very cold
and as he curled himself up and fell asleep, the big flakes of
snow fell steadily on his body.

Penny Robinson was returning from her music lesson with
her mother and was about to go through the gate when she
noticed the little heap of snow at her feet. She pushed at it
with her shoe, and, as she cleared the snow away with her
hand, she cried out in surprise.

'Oh, look, Mummy! There's a tiny dead lamb under the
snow!'

'A lamb? It can't be!' exclaimed Mrs Robinson.

Penny looked closer. 'It is, it is, and maybe he's not dead. I
think he's still breathing.'

S he picked Smudge up in her arms and hurried down the garden path. Inside the house she put him on the kitchen table where he lay very still with his eyes closed.

Penny brushed the snow from him and rubbed him with a towel, but he did not move and his wool stayed damp and bedraggled.

'We must get him warm or he'll die,' said Penny. Then she
had an idea. She ran up to the bedroom and fetched her
mother's hairdryer and began to blow warm air on to the
tiny body. Again and again she sent the heat from the dryer
from head to tail and back again, waiting for some signs of
life from the little creature.

From way down in the depths of his icy sleep, Smudge
became aware of the delicious warmth swirling around him
like a summer breeze, thawing him out, drying his wool,
pulling him back into the world. It was like a lovely dream -
as though he was back with his mother on the sunny
hillside field. When he opened his eyes and looked up into
Penny's face, she laughed in delight.

'Look, look, it's working! He's coming around!' She
continued using the dryer, fluffing up the wool until it
looked just the same as when Smudge had left the field. But
still the little lamb didn't move.

He's so weak, he needs some food,' Penny said. 'Where is the bottle I had when I was a baby?'

Mrs Robinson laughed and got the bottle from a cupboard, filled it with warm milk and gave it to Penny.

When Smudge felt the teat in his mouth he knew what to do. He had hardly any strength left, but he could still suck and the level in the bottle went down rapidly. Penny refilled the bottle and Smudge sucked again until his little stomach was full to bursting.

He began to feel much better and he looked around him at yet another strange place, the cosy kitchen with its cheerful fire. It was all new to him, but much better than the cold world outside.

Penny made a bed for him in a cardboard box by the fireside and he drifted into a deep contented sleep.

Next morning Penny was delighted to find him out of the box, and running round the room.

'What shall I do with him?' she asked her mother. 'He's so sweet – can I keep him as a pet?'

'I don't think that would be very convenient,' replied her mother. 'He's going to grow up into a big sheep and we only have a small garden. We must try to find out something about him.'

Penny gave him another bottle of milk and then went off to the school in the village.

When the teacher came in Penny put up her hand and told the class about the lamb she had found.

'Well, that is interesting,' said the teacher. 'I wonder where he came from.'

As she spoke, Harry Cobb, who was in Penny's class, put up his hand and jumped to his feet. 'Please, Miss, we lost a lamb yesterday. He was really my lamb, my father gave him to me, and he was missing when I got home from school.' He turned towards the girl and held out his hands. 'Is he about this size, Penny? And does he have a black face with a white mark on his nose?'

'Yes,' she replied.

'Well, that's Smudge! That's my lamb!'

After school that day, the snow had melted away and
Farmer Cobb went down to the village in his car to
collect Smudge. Penny went back to the farm with them,
and she and Harry watched as the little lamb was reunited
with his mother and sister in the sunny field.

They laughed as Smudge and Smartie pushed their heads
under the ewe and sucked happily, their little tails twirling.

'He's all right now, Penny, thanks to you,' Harry said. 'You
saved his life.'

Penny laughed. 'It was really the hairdryer that saved him.'

There was only one thought in Smudge's mind as he
enjoyed his mother's milk. This was where he wanted to be.
He would never ever try to get out of the field again.